Exile

Exile

Anita Barrows

Kelsay Books

ISBN-13: 978-0692366677

Cover art: Nora Barrows-Friedman

Kelsay Books
Aldrich Press
www.kelsaybooks.com

For Nora, Viva and Ciel

My deepest gratitude, as always, to my daughters Nora and Viva and my granddaughter Ciel, and to Joanna Macy. My conversations with each of you inform these words. Thanks also to Anita Price, Dawn McGuire, David Shaddock, Ellen Balis, Jack Schiemann, Chana Bloch, Bill Mayer, Joseph Stroud, Susan Griffin, Mary Laird, and Mariolina Freeth, all of whom saw and commented on various iterations of this work.

(1)

All afternoon you have been slicing carrots, onions, tomatoes,
pinching leaves of basil and oregano,

dropping them into a pan of oil
on the stovetop. The oil sizzles, the fragrance of your cooking

fills the apartment. You stand on the narrow balcony
off the kitchen, above the streets. A small bird,

sparrow or finch, comes to land
on the highest branch

of the sycamore across from you, which has just
this week come into leaf. Sapphire sky

between leaf-shapes, blue
deepening before it dissolves

into night. How
did this happen, that you have arrived

in a place of pavement and sycamores?
Who is it

that is coming to share this meal
with you? For which

of your ghosts
have you prepared this table?

(2)

At moments you stand on the parched asphalt
of this city you live in, dreaming ripe figs,

rooms where people are eating and talking,
nights soft as the hair just over a donkey's nostril.

Once there was a place
you would have belonged to forever,

of figs, night, donkeys. You dream your name
is the name of a mountain range. Spare

and essential, like granite. To pierce
the clear sky, to make deep moist shadows

beneath which—in cool
shadowy earth—those you have loved

could slake their thirst, could come to rest at last.

(3)

You walk the hillside
where fig trees are ripening,

sucking the red juicy pulp
from the black skin.

Your grandmother and grandfather
stumble behind you, though they are dead

all these years: they who had lived

in refugee camps, who died
of hunger or maybe of longing. They

are the darkness
pursuing you: even when you lie in bed

with a lover, they are with you,
eating the meager bread from your cupboard.

Speak to us, they say, or *feed us.*
They do not say *Avenge us,*

nor even *Never forget us.*

(4)

What you wanted to save
could not be saved: wild mornings

of wind and grasses, your mother's
laughter, the bird you never saw

who announced each dawn at your window
and then flew off. Who you are now

is as impenetrable
as the stone wall that stood

at the bottom of the field. All this you recall
as the scent of datura

permeates the night air: Datura,

its flared
white trumpets, poison

mingled with sweetness.

(5)

The single tree that remained in the garden
where the others were burned, stripped, hacked from their roots.

Today would have been the day
seeds filled the air like snow, flying east

on their weightless wings.
Instead there is one tree

with white blossoms, one memory.
Instead you stumble among the ruins of your life

to pull toward you
one flowering branch, bury your face in it, breathe in

some defiant abundance.

(6)

You could not bury the ones who died as the villages burned.
Trees writhed toward the sky, stars careened toward earth,

blazed in their ashes. You ran, looking only

at what was ahead: a road, a clearing.
The outlines of hills. Behind you

even the syllables of childhood were consumed in flame.

(7)

Who would harbor you
but these strangers? The one

who weighs the fruit you buy
at the market, talking about his daughters,

the weather, the cost of fixing his truck;
another who works in a shop

on the avenue, who hands you change,
tells you how beautiful your hair is, the color

of your coat.   What
do they know of you?   For the last hour

a bird has sat on the telephone pole
outside your window, a woodpecker

tapping messages to the missing.

(8)

How lonely the stars must be, your child said once:

out there in the night, living
at such vast distances from each other.

They shine as they perish. What joins them
to one another are threads of longing.

Minerals igniting minerals

far above darkened houses
where lives break apart each night or come together.

(9)

You wanted to be transparent.
Not to find but to be found. To speak words

spare and unadorned
like stones washed again and again by the sea.

(10)

You dream the fields
have burned down to nothing.

Their ash commingles

with the ashes of your house. Your life
blazes in the night and you

can do nothing to stop it. You wake, make coffee,

pull on an old sweater, open a door
that is no longer there. All you have lost

falls like a chaos of stars through your hands.

(11)

In the room where you slept,
newspaper, old scarves, socks

plugged bullet holes in the wall.

In that place where you were a girl,
a young woman waiting in line for food,

waiting in line for a piece of stamped paper—

in that place where you were a young mother
clutching a child's hand, taking shelter

in the doorways of strangers—

it is morning now. The friends who remained
sit at breakfast with other friends

at tables in other rooms

where walls are still patched
with towels and rags against the cold.

Save what can be saved.

(12)

There was a music you knew, hands that played it,
a woman's voice dark as an underground river.

You don't remember the words, only
that they carried you into sleep. Their current

was slow and certain, the strings
beneath the melody stretched

from this world to the next and back again.
They bore away hunger, argument, fear.

They returned accompanied by oranges and cicadas.
Sleep, sleep, the voice chanted, or *death, death,* or

everything you have lost will be restored.
Outside your window you heard leaves flutter

in the last breeze of night, and grow still.

(13)

Sitting on a balcony overlooking a city: this
is how you think of yourself, even

when you ride in the closed compartment
of a train, even when the syllables

of the language down there
in the streets are as foreign

to you as they were
at the start, even when you stand

at the stall in the market, watching
the scale where the fruit

you've chosen is being
weighed—even then

you are sitting, a woman with dark eyes,
on a slatted chair on a balcony,

the sky
turning a deep red-purple

before night comes with its inevitable chill.

(14)

The mirror does not give you back to yourself.
The mirror says you are last, first, what falls

to earth and streams in rivulets
down parched time, season and silt and sediment.

The mirror looks past you to those
who stood behind you, fields at their backs,

places where they took shelter
from rain or bullets, from planes

whose shadows chilled them
as they swept over them.

(15)

A precision the hand knows. Ungloved.
Unshielded. Peeling skin from a cucumber, or skillfully,

in an hour without bullets,
removing the splinter

from the child's hand. You note the way hand and eye

work together, see how
a moment can be infused with tenderness

when the child, sitting
on a bench in the schoolyard

in an hour free of the noises of war,
holds out the afflicted

thumb and you
take out the tweezers, place

them exactly, probe
until the bit of wood is loosened.

Or the cool discs of cucumber
falling from the knife's blade

into the bowl, dark skin dropping in curled
ribbons onto the countertop.

The meal will be eaten, evening will come, the child

will sleep in his bed. Oh most careful, most

ordinary, the world's
shining and aching, the hand's

swiftness, its nakedness. Every moment

to rescue the living.

(16)

Speak now about the child, the one who was walking
to school with his backpack, his blue sweater,

the one he hadn't wanted to wear because it was too warm.
Tell of the street that ended in barbed wire,

the garbage rotting there. Speak
of his mother—you—a block away,

wiping the table after breakfast, the last
tomato plants of the season

in their pots outside the window. The cars
going by, the soldiers. The soldiers

standing as they did every day
in the street, smoking and talking,

guns at their sides. One of them

standing apart from the others, holding
his gun and aiming. A quiet day.

The soldier's dark glasses, pressed uniform.
Tell now about the sound

that punctured the air, and then other sounds.

Tell how the child had blue canvas shoes, black socks,
a plastic truck in his backpack he was going to return

to a friend. Tell how the school day

was just beginning, while he lay—
alive! still alive!—

on the sidewalk, blood
staining his shoes, his backpack, his warm

blue sweater. His mother—
you—running toward him

from the house where everything
afterward would be measured by this.

(17)

In the waiting room at the hospital
you peel and eat oranges you've bought

the morning before at the market. A bag full of oranges.
Strange, how

the white rind
is bitter and then mysteriously sweet.

How the sections are crescents, how the peel if split

reveals that it too is juicy, though its juice
is sharp, emerges

as a fine spray. In the waiting room

at the hospital you make yourself
think about oranges

while the doctors operate on your child.

Blinking lights, electronic beeps, loudspeakers
summoning this name, then that.

How many hours have passed.
What news will come through the closed white doors.

How fragrant the blossoms
of the orange tree. You have known this

from childhood: how its fruit

hangs like globes among dark
leaves, how it begins in winter,

weighs down the branches.

(18)

When your friend must go you do not ask him
where he is going. You offer him

chilled lemonade with a sprig
of mint. You drink

together. He turns,

walks down the stairs. You hear
a car door opening, an engine igniting, tires

grinding against the pebbled road.
You rinse the glasses, set them to dry

on a cloth on the tile counter.   You put out seed

for the birds who will come
to the window. Somewhere south of you

he drives
through a landscape of bleached grass, ruined houses.

Their long shadows. The lives of others.

The objects
of your solitude

console you a little
in late afternoon light.

(19)

Who does not plant trees will not harvest the fruit.

Who does not offer her life will not live.
Who does not scatter seeds, water them,

watch them push through the soil—green, tentative,
bowed by rain, wind

scorched by the heat of the day—

who does not wait
for the moment

when what has been closed will open,
when what holds itself back

will yield, bend, embrace,
grow heavy, swell with juices—

who does not pluck the fruit will not eat,
will not lie down at night

under the dome of stars, nor come
at last to the table.

(20)

Walking home, holding a heavy basket of pears.
Evening is coming, lamps will be lit in the houses.

You are thinking
about your child: how he will smile

when he sees the ripe pears, how
he will hold the ripest one

in both his hands, and bite
into the skin. How the juice

will run down his chin, his fingers.
Across the fields the sun

is setting, the sky is the color
of russet pears.

(21)

In the hospital waiting room
outside the white doors

to the corridor that leads to the room
where your child lies, the great lights over him.

The surgeons and their exact instruments.
The child's small inexact hands that this morning

were caked with mud from the road—
antiseptically cleaned, lying still for once.

(22)

In whose hands
will you place your trust?

With which of these strangers
in this waiting room

would you break bread?

With the woman asleep, face
hidden, shawl over her lap?

Or the woman attempting to read a newspaper,
never turning the page, now and again sighing loudly.

Tonight it could be your names
in the tense brief paragraphs

You want to ask her
who she is waiting for, what kind of day she had

that ended here.

(23)

A wind from the west, bearing the scent of the sea.
The new grass blows on the hillside, reminds you

of flocks of sheep, waves, of the delicate hair
on the arm of a child. Out there

where sea and sky
finally meet

one bird

threads its way, sewing together
what has been and what might become.

(24)

How many times did you sit
on the stone steps of your house

watching soldiers
stride up the road?

How many times did you see
snipers' bullets hitting the wall

of the house next to yours, or the school, or the pavement?

Sometimes the soldiers were pointing at you.
Sometimes they were pointing at someone you couldn't see.

Once, after a round of shots, you saw a tomato

ripened on its stem
in the small garden your mother tended

fall to the ground, just like that,
skin unbroken.

(25)

It's all finished now, says the mother
of the dead child, the mother

who sits in the waiting room
across from you all night, the one

who was trying to read
the paper: the mother of the boy

not as lucky as yours, the boy
who had been studying

for his algebra exam
when shots were fired

through his bedroom window. It's all
finished now, the anxiety

over grades, the notebooks

with their crossed-out words, the dreams
of being a doctor, an engineer.

Later his mother will hold a paper

in her hands: algebra problems
perfectly done, the last one

unfinished. Columns
neatly aligned, equations

computed so everything arrives
at the desired sum.

(26)

Dimensions of light: a strong wind
herding grass up the hillside, showing the silver

undersides of leaves. Even the stony ground
you came from

yielded jewels in the sunlight,
shifted from gold to red to blue.

Never to stop
resisting. To stake the tent of your being

over and over
despite the roar

of helicopters overhead,
the grim syncope

of gunfire, the certainties of loss.

(27)

A telephone rings; a voice answers

from a machine, your friend's voice
that from today on will never speak any words

but these. Some days you will call the number
twice, three times, once even a dozen times. Sooner or later

the line will be disconnected. Another voice, indifferent,
will say there is no new number. Then one day

a stranger will answer, to whom the number
will have been reassigned.

You'll say nothing to him. It will be the last call.
He will not know

the story you are only beginning to believe. For now
you allow yourself this game, this small defiance.

Death can't take everything, you say, dialing
the familiar number, waiting for the ring, the click, the words.

(28)

Everything might be a waiting room,
you tell yourself, or a door.

You remember an afternoon

when you and your child and your friend
who was killed

went walking beside the sea.
A sunny windy day. February? March?

Terns. Plovers. Tips of foam

riding the waves
playfully, like your steps

playful in wet sand. The memory

alights for an instant
like a bird, a shorebird. And is gone.

(29)

What does it matter
what names we were given

when we take off
this apron of flesh, this rag of history?

A tree
bursts into flame,

 a girl walking along the road

shields her face
with her hand, runs until she sees

she has escaped. With what?
Flame. Flame

answering flame. We are bodies

of light, voices

pleading to be heard

over the roar
of everything that is burning.

(30)

A fistful of earth. Severed roots,
corpses of insects.

What is the speed of the sky
as it moves among branches? Whose hand

do you remember in yours
when you hold the lemon

you've just now picked? Oh the stones,

the dry clods of dirt, the leaves
twisting in wind that blows

from the south. These,
these drops of bitter juice

that fall into the glass—
is this your country?

(31)

The child's bones have been cleaned
as much as possible of shrapnel,

set, fastened again

one to another as they were
when he turned within you. The surgeon

shows them to you
on the x-ray screen.

How solid they are. Not hollow,
you think, like flutes

or birds' bones. Though this

is how music happens; this
is how birds can fly. And a child

can't fly, because his bones
are made of struggle and dread;

though now and again they too,
for a moment,

can lift him above your
troubled sleep, your uneasy turning.

(32)

Don't let those whose hands
have bound your hands

tell you which road to walk,
which fruit

to pluck from the tree.
Don't most stories

turn at some point to where one
who is loved is lost, wanders

in forest or desert while everything
left behind grows barren? Aren't your songs

all songs of resistance, don't you hold
in your hands the memory of what

once held them tenderly, passionately?
Even bound, even broken, aren't they hands

that know harvest and earth and return?

(33)

You think sometimes
you are a field

where wind twists and flattens the grass.
In a doorway down there in the street

an old gray cat who belongs
to no one is sleeping. It's clear

she won't live long. Who will remember her

but those like you
who have fed her, witnessed

her bird-dance, rat-dance....With whom

will you grieve her passing?

(34)

Your mother went into the garden
each morning, picked flowers

for the table. A flower bloomed every day
among cheeses and bread, boiled eggs and coffee.

You sat eating, a child whose feet
barely reached the floor.   What

did you know of her life? Who are you
to say she was lonely?

(35)

It's not clear
to you anymore

how the roads connected
to each other, how it was possible

to walk from your village
to the next

where a woman your mother knew
had pears for you from her orchard,

a story to tell you, a dress
she had made for you of blue cotton cloth.

You knew how to walk there
because you had always walked there.

You knew where to sit
in her kitchen, how to wait

while she served you cold tea
with a sprig of mint,

a little almond cake she had baked.

You remember the pears: how
you would eat one or two

on the way home
as evening was falling. Golden light

and then blue and

the heavy basket of
pears, green and golden.

(36)

There will be words

to redeem these losses, but not
now, not yet. You look out

from your balcony
over the streets, the streaming

cars. The sky

is the color of childhood.   The color
of russet pears.

(37)

There are nights you wait for the dead
to speak, and they do. You trust them.

What they tell you is truth if not solace.
Awake or asleep, you are always listening.

And you remember passing your grandmother's room,
hearing her weep for her dead sons.

One son. Two. Three. With each name
she accused the Infinite.

They were your uncles. You remember them
tall and limber, like young trees.

(38)

Your life is a music in a crowded cafe.

Tables where people bend their heads
toward each other,

conversation circled by conversation, chill air
near the open door, strong smell of coffee.

You are stirring your life into another's. You are drinking the sky.

The streets' dampness clings to you today.
You sit, slowly eating some sweet cake.

Give me breath, my song,
sings the woman over there

in the corner with her guitar, *as I have given breath to you.*

(39)

Those who loved you have gone on before you.
Where they stood, the shadows of trees grow long.

Soon the sky over the vacant lots of the city
will be strewn with stars.

Small purposeful rodents scurry back and forth

under mounds of dirt. Can you hear
them? You who still live

in this world, suspended

between the galaxies' darkness
and the darkness of tunnels under the earth.

(40)

You come after all these years to this
hour before evening, this softest hour.

Birds settle restlessly in the trees. The sky
gathers the colors of day into the last color.

You walk out on your balcony
among potted plants whose flowers

are closing.
Lights appear

in the windows
as stars appear, each by each.

Another day of history is finished.

(41)

Your life is the story of more than exclusion.
You were standing against a wall, a stone wall—

its coolness, its roughness through the thin cotton
of your dress. A woman walked by,

carrying a child. A mother, tired
at the end of day, walking toward home.

The afternoon returns to you: jasmine, oleander,
the broad leaves' shadows.

You were eating some full
summer fruit, its juice streaking your arm to the elbow.

You licked the sweetness from your fingers.

(42)

A wind from the sea blows the branches of the orange tree
against the stucco wall of the house.

Night wind. Your hand

reaches for the window, pushes it open.
Eyes closed, you breathe in a fragrance of salt and oranges.

There have been years

like oranges
fallen too soon from the branch, rotted

before they were tasted.

(43)

The dead are not lost. They are oranges
ripening on a branch.

When you dream, they are beside you,
more real than the mild night air.

Try and count them. Their number
goes up in flame like everything else,

descends to earth again, ash
indistinguishable from fallen blossoms.

(44)

A horse stands near another horse

at the edge of a field, at the edge of the city.

You stand across the road from them, watching them
from the other side of language. Now

there are others, their long necks

lowered, noses wet
with the wetness of cooling grass. The horses know

what they will return to: the warm
stable smelling of hay. What you belong to

lives far from you or within you and cannot be touched.

(45)

You would climb just now
over that split-rail fence

to where the horses

graze, ask their permission
to be among them. Their long

necks lowered. The damp
grass, the sound of their eating. Instead

you stand watching.
Slowly the horses

begin to move
toward the other end of the pasture. Slowly

the seam that binds this world to the other
splits open a little. You glimpse what is there.

(46)

You begin to build a house of your unknowing.
Can the sky stretch wide enough

to encompass it? Will the tools you have brought

be enough? Here is a roof of forgetting,
a wall made of bones and grief. You touch

the door; it comes apart in your hands
like old paper

on which something is written
that flakes away. A bird

threads its way through the evening
calling in a shrill insistent voice as it flies,

Not for you, not for you, not for you.

(47)

Those who loved you have gone on before you.
Even the friend who never wanted to leave your side

is dust and wind. In this spring morning

all the voices of your life
are calling your name.

You pick up a handful of soil
from a vacant lot, smell

the ripe rich smell of earth,
the same earth everywhere.

(48)

Uprooted. Dirt

clung to you
as you ran.

The same
history

bent you
and the trees

to its bitter need.

(49)

Come, put away the food you have bought.
Heat up the coffee left over from breakfast.

You, who thought
you had run out of words. You, solitary; you

who like to say you're without desire.
What is this story you want suddenly to tell?

What if you've been summoned here
simply as witness?

(50)

A window uphill, singled out
by the last light of day.

It blazes and then is absorbed into darkness.

What love or anger or sorrow
flared in that room? And who,

looking sometime at the window
where *you* sit, lit by such chance,

will ask herself who it is
who lives there, engulfed for a moment in radiance?

(51)

You are not permitted to cross this border.
You have no papers, no letter, no identity card

and this is a country that does not issue passports
because its name changes every hour, and its language

is spoken by no one

but those
who are learning to forget.

(52)

The light in your window is part of a constellation
that tells a story of work and time and refuge.

Of subways and cafes, of walking upstairs
after a day of papers and talk,

of the smells of cooking and washing, the clean smell
of sheets folded back at the end of day. Once you lay

between sheets, touching your child's fine hair.
Now he phones you from a city

you've never seen, though the ocean that starts at the edge
of your avenues ends where he can see it from his window.

You warm the coffee left over from breakfast, sit
for a moment before the tasks of evening begin.

Something like gratitude
overcomes you, you don't know how.

(53)

Will the world need these words?
What did you tell the child

of the lives you had already buried,
covering everything with earth

so death might be concealed, so death
might avert its eyes from you?

(54)

The door closes, the friends who came for the evening
go, taking their laughter with them.

Glasses half-filled with wine
still stand on the table. A novel

one of them brought you, a bunch of violets
from somebody's garden. Once you were anchored

to earth by nothing except a child's breath.
Warplanes buzzed overhead, fruit

went on ripening. You moved through a landscape
of blunted promises. *This is the world,*

you said to the child. *This isn't the world.*

(55)

Mornings you walk to the market
carrying empty bags that soon

will be filled with greens, asparagus, early strawberries.
In the high branches of sycamores: sparrows, finches.

You peer up into the light, see them
only as movement. *Look,* you say

silently to the crowded street, *we remain alive
in a world that sings.*

(56)

You, restless. You, always turned
toward what might be coming.

Do you think your stories are new?
Haven't parents always been carried

through dark underground worlds
on the backs of their children? Are you ashamed

that the child's hand comforts you?
He does not know who called you inside

when the first stars
appeared over the roofs. He does not remember

the stammer of bullets against stone walls,
frantic braying of donkeys. What do you tell him

when you turn out the light? That the grass
is innumerable, but sorrows

appear, disappear, blur into each other
like drops of rain on a window?

(57)

Planes pass overhead on their deadly errands.
It is the year you are learning to read.

You trace the paths in the sky
with your finger: over the high trees, over the roofs

of the known houses, out toward the fields
you don't know, out toward the city

you've never seen. And the story
you trace with your finger

in the cloth-bound book
unfolds: a smiling child

in an unbroken world.

(58)

Hours waiting in line
for papers with the right official words.

Holding the child's hand in the airport.
His silence and yours, as the loudspeaker announced

flights that were not your flight and finally
one that was. Looking down

as the plane rose and tilted
over the bruised land

that had been yours: roads, houses

where people were going about their day
as though it were a day like any other.

Fields where, in spite of everything,
trees might blossom again and bear fruit.

(59)

What you know is that there is nothing
you can keep safe, and this knowledge

assails you when you wake, your whole body
shaking though the apartment is peaceful

and the child sleeps peacefully in his small bed next to yours
and the city you have come to is not a city of war.

You know there is something you need to say
and you know you will never be able to say it

because it is unsayable, even as your love
for the sleeping child is unsayable

and vast as the ocean at the end of the avenues.

(60)

Will you set down what you've carried, now that you can?
I'm so happy, your son says, calling

on his cell phone as he walks beside a bay
traversed with sailboats on a sparkling morning

in a city he's visiting. He whose legs
are still scarred where they pulled the shrapnel

out—doesn't he walk in long strides, lover
at his side, voice

strong, words unambiguous? *So happy*

he says, and you tell him
how light you feel, suddenly, as though

you could skim lightly as a boat
over the sorrows of your life.

(61)

Tonight you remember the child with the bullet in his head.
He was not your child, he was someone's child

who happened to be walking to school at the wrong
time. The day before he'd been fighting

with a friend over a basketball.

What does the friend remember of him?
The wild wrestling to the cement?

The cry, "Enough!"
as fingers locked, one arm twisted behind the head—

which a day later
would never turn again.

Which some soldier—someone

else's child—would stand over
with his gun in the street

watching the boy's eyes grow still, the mouth
twitch and grow still.

Classmates opening their books in the schoolroom.
The basketball forgotten in the corner of the yard.

(62)

Resist the soldier who kicks the boy to the ground
and shoots him at point blank range.

Resist the tanks, the engines driving the tanks,
the voices of advisors advising the tank drivers.

Resist the voices of certainty, they are not your voices.
They say *danger,* they say *no danger*. They say *lives*

have been lost but they were not our lives. They say
these losses were necessary. They say *think*

of the things we must save, aren't we saving them?

(63)

Impossible not to remember

the dog who came out
of the yard where he lived

every morning to greet you

in the years no one else
seemed to know your name.

He was a dog, you
were a woman, passing. *Hello dog,*

you would say
silently or in your own language

and he, silently
or in his own language

would reply, *Hello woman.* You belonged equally
to the trees, the budding or fallen leaves.

Salt smell, muffled sunlight of a coastal city.

(64)

Each of us is a drop of moisture in the eye of the infinite.

You repeat this to yourself as you go through the day
wondering if it's a phrase from an old prayer

or maybe a poem you heard in childhood
or some song you half-heard on the radio this morning

as you washed the dishes.

Old or new, whether or not
you believe it,

you find it comforting
as you walk through the chilly rooms, the lonely hallway.

(65)

To what sorrow have you tuned your instrument?
Whose mourning weeps in your voice?

To take the hands of the child, to warm them between your own.
To warm your hands with your own breath and feel

those who loved you breathing through you.
You are a reed, a string, a carved stick of wood

through which the years play a melody

you half forget, though your lips
and your fingers have shaped themselves to it.

(66)

When words failed, your hands were strong.
All afternoon you carried buckets of water

up from the river. You washed blood
from the tiles on the floor, the stairs, the doorposts.

The sun shone after days of rain.
Birds sang as though nothing had happened.

You used a long stick with a cloth at the end of it
torn from some piece of clothing.

Only the day before you were still a child.

(67)

Do the birds sense what happens
beneath the currents of air they ride?

The vastness they breathe
is pierced by wires, antennas.

You feed them. They alight for moments
on the balcony rail. You take pleasure in them

for their slightness, their vigilance. For the way
they balance on a strip of wrought iron

two fingers wide
between your world and their own.

(68)

The savaged earth yields what it yields.
Do you have all your tools? Can you dig, scrape, uproot?

These cracks in the soil
were made by time and drought.

By those whose feet
ran desperately over it. By those who couldn't run.

You don't believe the earth will split
to reveal stories you have forgotten,

but still you come in your dreams
after all these years

to uncover what's there.

(69)

Somewhere perhaps one horse

still stands at the edge of a field.
Is he, too, dreaming his life?

Does he remember sunlight pouring between leaves,
a road alive with voices?

(70)

Each by each the stars are absorbed by daylight.
It is only their light obscured

by a brighter, nearer light. So it is with you now
as you go through your day, trying to remember those

from the gone years: their faces
not clear to you, though you know

they will return to you
when night comes.

Night that gathers everything to itself.

(71)

What was the texture of the child's hair?
Didn't he walk beside you

for years, vibrant, curious? Everything
is lost, though you might say

that nothing is lost. The child he was
is gone, the child you were

is a wisp of blue cotton fluttering in a breeze
from a sea that is not the one

at the end of your avenues.

(72)

Neither mystery nor clarity lightens your hours,
but a yellow finch who comes to you

just when you thought no one would come again.
What you hoped for was someone

to share a glass with you, sit with you
on your balcony for hours into the night,

speaking sometimes and sometimes silent.   Instead

what you have is a yellow finch
alighting there

on the rail,
singing over and over

I leave, I return.

(73)

There was a house on a road in a village,
an ochre house with trees that rose past the windows.

And in the trees, birds
whose names you still know

only in your own language, after all

these years. And the house is fallen, the ruins
of its walls exposed

to sun and rain and night and finally
the wrecker's tools, a pile

of stones and wood boys use in their games of war
on long afternoons.

(74)

Your heart was emptied again and filled again

as leaves broke off
from their branches and fell, as pebbles

turned smooth and polished,
as light made mottled patterns

changing and changing again on stone. Yellow and purple
wildflowers

sprang up from the dust of midafternoon

even beneath the shadows of warplanes
even in fields of husk and bone.

(75)

You walk out in a chill wind,

press your face to white petals of magnolia, breathe in
something you feel you were promised.

Down the street children are kicking a ball
to each other in the last light of day.

If summer is only
what happened long ago—

if the languor of heat, the glare
of the sea at noon, are nothing but memory,

will not come to you again, can you forgive
whatever there is to forgive

and breathe in this tenacity of blossoms

that seemed as though they would fall to earth
when you touched them,

and yet did not?

(76)

The day bequeaths you sunlight and exile,
strong coffee and fingers raw from cold.

You are traversed by lives gone beyond your reach.
You want to hold them, to speak of them

to the man selling apples, the children
laughing as they step onto the schoolbus, the yellow dog

who keeps pace with you for a while, then returns
to the doorstep where he had been sleeping.

(77)

On your kitchen wall, the last shadows of day.
A tree weaves itself into other trees, shapes

appear, disappear. Evening will come
and fold everything into itself,

and yourself with everything.

Gone in an instant
the last streak of light, conversations of birds. Gone

the small hope of the hour: whatever it was
that flickered or sang to you

from across the avenues.

(78)

Once your child ran to you, his hands
full of plums he had picked from the neighbor's garden.

The red stains on his fingers startled you, but it was sweetness
you kissed there, life abounding in him and not death.

Ripening plums catch the light on the tree
at the edge of the courtyard, where now the children

are playing some game of tag, some call and response.
The sunlight that falls

on the plums
falls across your hands. How it works

on the interiors of things, how it softens,
sweetens the fruit.

(79)

You prepare the rooms
as though a guest were coming, as though

you were waiting for someone you loved

who would speak, now and then
taking your hand, now and then

stopping to look out the window
to think about what had just been said.

The night sky is sown with stars like seeds.
No one is about to come

to your table, and yet you are filled.

(80)

Once you ran from an upstairs room in the house
where you were a child

to meet your grandmother on the road. She called your name.

It was summer: long afternoons filled with waiting
and the ceaseless buzzing of insects.

The bag she was carrying overflowed
with what she had bought at the market.

You remember the tiles of the stairs,

the cool passageway
to the door and the assault

of heat. You remember taking the bag from her,
heavier than you had imagined, and how the dusty earth then

seemed to rise and press into the soles of your feet.

(81)

The bag of vegetables you took
from your grandmother's hands.

The sound of oil
sizzling in a pan on the stove. A blue cotton dress

you wore, that you had already outgrown,
but which you loved for the ribbons

that ran along its hem. A white cup
your mother gave you to drink from

the time you lay in bed for weeks
with a fever. A cat whose tail

had been ripped by the teeth
of a fox, who walked

proudly among the rooms
of the house, holding that stump aloft. Pods

of cardamom in your father's
coffee: how you took one

in your mouth, broke it open, swallowed

the too-strong
pungent seed.

(82)

The fields were in flames, the house
with its tile hallways had ribbons of flame

twisting out of its upstairs windows. Did the trees
explode? Or is that only the way

you remember it, smoke more black
than any black you had seen, a roar

behind you: wind
bearing fire through the leaves

 of all the trees you had ever known.

(83)

Did you find clarity in grief? Did the years
run together like droplets of rain on a window?

Were there voices that spoke to you,
hands that stretched toward you, palms open,

waiting for whatever you had to offer?
Did the rain stop one day without your noticing

and suddenly sunlight spill over the furniture?
Did you beg not to forget? Did you put on your coat and go out

into the living street? Do you still
hold grief before your eyes

like a fine-ground lens through which the living
resemble the dead?

(84)

From the dead children's bones nothing can be made.
Maybe stories can be made if you think of the words.

You don't know where they're buried, you don't know
if the bodies in the little graves are theirs. That's how

they died, too: indistinguishable from each other.

There were books stained with blood but you threw them away.
There were notebooks

with their young penmanship, words that ran outside the lines.

Your child was the one who lived, just as you
were the one who ran from the burning house.

Is this the story you're telling? How at last
you decided to take him away,

taking nothing with you, and less

than nothing, leaving even the words behind,
the stale smell of wind carrying all those ashes?

(85)

Do the roots of the fig trees
grope toward each other,

or have they died,
like everything else you knew, into

the soil? The dry soil

that all day drinks in light and heat
and offers it back

through your restless nights as memory,
as memory of memory.

(86)

Yellow finches fly out of the tangle of trees.
The fruit hangs ripe and the color of sunrise.

Are you ready to take what falls? Are you ready to gather
whatever sharpness and sweetness

lie inextricable on the parched ground?

(87)

To be remembered by leaves, to be recognized

by a wind that travels across the grasses:
to belong to the house you escaped, though where it stood

only charred beams remain, broken tiles.

(88)

All day you hammer shut the windows

of a silenced house, a house you loved
that doesn't exist.

Close up everything, everything!

As though everything might be kept safe—

the child fed, the horse
tethered in the field,

the gate secured.

(89)

The telephone rings, your child who is now a man

is calling from where it is morning. He is standing
at the window, looking out over the harbor.

Waves move across the hours
between your city and his. News of the life

he is living.   Beneath the words, the unspoken message:
We have endured; and you reply

(though your words
are about the things of the day), *We have endured.*

(90)

To have lived between one siege and the next
and now walk the avenues at sunset,

watching those who return from the day's work
or those who, arm-in-arm, walk into a cafe....

The last light of day shines on the wall
of the building you live in, makes it glow

deep crimson, as though lit from within.

What has it taken for you
to feel, from time to time, such simple happiness?

(91)

Inside your apartment

lamps are lit, books stacked on the table,
the radio plays a Mozart quintet. This is not

the world you were given
but it is the world you have.

What you wanted was heat,

light, the deep blue of the fig at the end of summer,
sweet weight of oranges pulling down the branch.

The last bird rises from the sycamore,

the quintet reaches a moment where the cello
follows one violin in a reprise of longing. *Take off,*

take off your mantle of ashes. Sit now and taste the fruit.

(92)

Your hands
trace on the table the arc of a life, yours

or another's: chaos and forgotten love, shafts of light,
grass willing to bear your weight.

You've learned to measure everything
by departures: a bird

flying out of the sycamore, a child taking

your hand, then running ahead. A place suddenly
empty of his shape, empty of even the sound

of his running. A beach at low tide
where together you gathered shells and stones:

the broad empty darkening sand
between your footprints and the sea's beginning.

(93)

What you took from the earth will be restored.
What you borrowed from this mild night air

will be given back in words or in song.
For centuries you will lie under the stars:

Pleas, praise, argument
will fall through your fingers

and be reabsorbed into the soil.
The shifting moods of the day will be as water

darkening under clouds, growing clear again.
You are nothing more

than a crossroads, a bend in the path.

Yet here you are on this moonless night,
having worked, eaten,

spoken a few words of love
and a few of disappointment.

So what if all journeys end in loss.

About the Author

Among Anita Barrows' awards in poetry have been grants from the National Endowment for the Arts, the Ragdale Foundation, the Dorland Mountain Arts Colony, and publications by the Quarterly Review of Literature and the Riverstone Press. Her poetry chapbooks from Quelquefois Press in Berkeley are housed, among other places, in libraries in Baghdad, Kabul, and in The British Museum. Barrows' translation, with Joanna Macy, from the German of *Rilke's Book of Hours* was nominated for a PEN Translation Award, and they have collaborated on two other translations of Rilke's work. Barrows has also done translations for British and American publishers of poetry, fiction, non-fiction and plays from French and Italian. She holds a PhD in psychology and is a professor of psychology at The Wright Institute, Berkeley. She maintains a private clinical practice in Berkeley and is a mother and grandmother and companion to a menagerie of dogs, cats and birds.